Let the Bud of Life Bloom

Let the Bud of Life Bloom

A Guide to Raising
Happy and Healthy Children

SWAMI RAMA

Himalayan Institute Hospital Trust
Swami Rama Nagar, P.O. Doiwala
Distt. Dehradun 248140, Uttarakhand, India

Acknowledgments

We would like to express our gratitude to Connie Gage for designing the cover, and to Wesley Van Linda for the guidance and inspiration so generously given to help make this venture possible.

Editing: Dr. Barbara Bova
Cover Design: Connie Gage

©2002 by the Himalayan Institute Hospital Trust
First USA and Indian edition, 2002
Second Indian edition, 2008
ISBN 978-81-88157-04-4
Library of Congress Control Number: 2002108354
Printed in India at Shiva Offset Press

Published by:

Himalayan Institute Hospital Trust
Swami Rama Nagar, P.O. Doiwala
Distt. Dehradun 248140, Uttarakhand, India
Tel: 91-135-241-2068, Fax: 91-135-247-1122
src@hihtindia.org; www.hihtindia.org

CONTENTS

FOREWORD

One of the most loveable aspects of Swamiji's personality was his child-like character, which would inevitably surface in the company of children. His love for children was unconditional. They likewise returned his love without hesitation and were uninhibitedly overjoyed when given an opportunity to be in his presence. He often remarked to the parents that the children are always better than their parents.

In the twenty-five years that Swamiji spent in the West he closely observed the American people and their lifestyles. *Let the Bud of Life Bloom* is an unpublished manuscript written by Swamiji in the early 80's to express his deep concern over the disintegration of the family institution and the loss of the basic training so necessary to children, not only in the West, but also in the East. The criticism and advice that Swamiji gives in this book are even more pertinent today for parents throughout the world since the process of globalization has become more widespread. Swamiji's unconditional love for children and his conviction that children are our hope for the future are evident throughout the book. His very straight-forward comments resonate from a deep and passionate concern for the welfare and future of humanity as a whole.

A few notes from Swamiji's lectures have been added to enhance the original manuscript.

INTRODUCTION

CULTURAL HERITAGE has a profound impact on human destiny because it leaves a deep imprint on the human mind and heart. Human culture is like an ocean with billions of waves: religion, philosophy, tradition, art, and history. Each individual floats within the cultural ocean like a tiny iceberg. Three-fourths of the individual's personality remains hidden underneath, while only a small part is known to oneself and to others. These tiny icebergs shatter against one another and finally dissolve. This ocean is the cosmos in which we live; it belongs to Providence. It is a manifestation of the fundamental truths over which we human beings build a world. We suffer, not because Providence wants us to suffer, but because of our way of life and our attachment to the floating, fleeting, and glittering objects of the world. Misery and strife are not the creations of Providence but of humanity. This is why the seers of the Upanishads cried, "Remove this glittering veil so that we can see the face of Truth." This cry is futile if one persists in living in a self-created world full of pain and misery.

Culture is like a work of art that has been painted with numerous colors by countless painters over many generations; it is like a colorful tapestry that has been woven for centuries and passed on from generation to generation by every society. Its colors intermingle to make an exquisite weaving that cannot easily be separated for analysis and study. Similarly, the human personality is a colorful tapestry that is woven of many habit patterns. A habit is a groove created by repeated actions. The word *personality* comes from its root, *persona*, a Greek word meaning "mask." We behave according to our personality. Our childhood personality is the strongest personality that we carry with us. All that is good or bad in the adult human being is the result of childhood habits.

I am one who has been observing human culture. I have studied cultural behavior and traditional hang-ups; I have examined the environments in which modern children are raised, and how children develop problems in childhood. I have come to the conclusion that most of our problems are sown in our childhood. We look the way we are and the way we are is mainly the product of our childhood education. If we have many fears in childhood and we learn to be meek and weak, later in life we will not be able to help ourselves. I have seen highly intellectual people, even those who are considered to be very great, become uneasy in the evening when the sun sets because they are afraid of ghosts. In their childhood they had been taught that there are ghosts who are very powerful, who can hurt and harm you, and even kill you. Even if someone tries to understand and analyze this ghost business, he will not be able to convince the unconscious. The seeds of belief that are sown in childhood become the guiding principles of the adult.

2

Human culture seems to be stuck in a pool of stagnant habits that are preventing civilization from attaining the next step of progress. Most of us live to please others, rather than living the way we want to live. This creates multiple personalities. We go on using false masks, one over the other. As a result, even our closest friends, relatives, and associates, can never know us. We do not even know ourselves. Although multiple personalities are sometimes considered to be creative aspects, actually they are not. Today if a person is a poet, orator, dancer, musician, and artist, he is considered to be versatile. But how many people are able to adjust to the many facets of their various personalities and integrate all of them into one? This is rarely seen. In order to comprehend and analyze the human personality one needs to understand life in its totality.

Society is wrapped in the ancient rags of useless customs and traditions that foster selfishness. Tradition and truth are two distinct realities. Tradition is not truth nor does it encourage growth. Relying on tradition, the ignorant find delight in their self-created whirlpools of misery. It is difficult to go beyond the traditional influences that develop from childhood onward; they remain until the last breath of human life. In India traditional values are given more importance than the realities of day-to-day life. This has been a great curse for our society. Even today we are not ready to change our traditional values that are blended with selfishness, attachment, and sense gratification. We have become a society of orthodoxy, and that orthodoxy has guided the destiny of our society toward isolation. Feeling that our values are superior, we have resisted the full exchange of cultural ideas. We are like a lake that supplies water to others but never accepts any stream to fill it. We dissipate our time and energy on rigid rituals and beliefs that were not born out of the philosophical truths of our ancients, but out of the dogmas created by selfish and egotistical leaders who knew little and commited self-centered errors. They have created a fool's paradise for our society, and our noble heritage has been lost. The custodians of our culture have become rigid, and the whole framework of society has become so enveloped by tradition that our view of the clear, clean horizon is obstructed. How can anyone grow without having a clear and clean vision of infinite space? The memories of the noble past have been recorded and carefully preserved in the many libraries of India to remind us of our noble heritage. Yet, we remain lost in pseudo-cultural habits and have developed into a society that is a mixture of the new and the old, without understanding the value of either. We have forgotten that our children are the rising generation of India that can shape a new nation and help to recover the losses of the past.

I have observed that in both the East and the West the upbringing of children has not been carefully designed. Many modern social problems have resulted from a lack of appropriate training in childhood. The institution of family life needs reformation. Parents no longer understand the importance of raising a child. It is time we develop a curriculum that will teach the values and responsibilities of family life. This type of education is missing in our homes today and is not imparted in any schools of the world. Unless we devise some new methods of training for our children that are not based on blind injunctions, the future of mankind will remain in peril. Our children will not become explorers, inventors, discoverers, or good citizens; they will not learn to communicate with each other. Communication is the essence of relationship. Without communication individuals cannot become part of, or help to create, an integrated society. When society disintegrates, the results are violence and destruction. Only an integrated society can produce peace, prosperity, and progress.

To raise a child in a healthy way requires a blend of the best of our ancient values and our new inventions. Our ancestors allowed their children to grow freely and offered help only when it was needed. It was a unique way for children to learn. The modern way of bringing up children has many serious defects because parents are selfish and care for their own pleasures more than for their children's welfare. I wonder why parents today do not make sacrifices for their children and allow them to grow according to their own potentials.

A swami has many children. I love them all madly and I generally speak for them because they are searching and they are trying to understand. This is particularly true about the younger generation in America. They are seeking, but I do not find discipline in them. After ten years they will be the custodians of their country. This fact has been forgotten. Because today's children all over the world will be the fathers and mothers of the next generation, society should provide all children with a complete education in how to be a human being. Now, let us examine how children are brought up in our society today.

CHAPTER ONE

FAMILY LIFE

FAMILY LIFE is a training ground for children to learn to relate to others from the very beginning. If that training ground is disturbed, the children will also be disturbed and will remain so throughout their whole life. The education that is imparted by colleges and universities definitely has some use. But a child who has not been raised in a good family atmosphere, even after having attained the highest education, will not know how to relate to others.

There are some fundamental differences between family life in Eastern culture and family life in the West. Until recently family life in the East has been a higher calling and a more profound and meaningful experience than in the West. But the East has been gradually forgetting the true values of life that the ancient architects of its great culture had cultivated. The family institution of Eastern society still has many good points, but the beautiful, ancient cultural values of the East are slowly being overwhelmed by the irresistible charms of the modern world. Indian culture has many good qualities, and those qualities are the binding forces that keep families united. In Eastern culture, and especially in India, children are given abundant love and attention because most of the mothers are not working mothers. Those mothers who do work arrange for some member of the family to care for and look after the children. Babysitting in the East is not the same as babysitting in the West. In India relatives in the household, especially the grandmothers, are the family's babysitters and raise the children. It is not acceptable to a child's heart and mind to be handed over to a stranger.

Closeness between parent and child is deeper in India than in any other culture. However, this closeness can grow into attachment, and the misery that accompanies attachment can create obstacles for both parents and child. Our scriptures say, "Do not be attached. Learn to love." We do not comprehend the meaning of these words because we are caught in the snares of attachment, and love remains unfulfilled. We suffer because we use many crutches, such as, "This is mine, this is mine, and this is mine." This "mine-ness" leads us to an illusory sense of ownership and causes us to sink and vanish into the swamp of possessiveness and attachment. Indian children lack self-confidence because of their parents' overpro-tectiveness and attachment to them. This is a serious defect in family life in India. Indian parents foolishly become attached to their children and impose their ideas and expectations on them.The children are expected to literally follow in the footsteps of their parents and to revere their parents more than necessary. They are not allowed to speak, to express themselves, or to think according to their natural inclinations, but instead are taught to accept their parents' ideas without any questioning or reasoning. Because of this lack of communication between the parents and the children, the children feel a lifelong pressure to live up to their parents' expectations. This constricted interaction hinders the development of the children's own talents and personality, and the potentials for development become stunted by fear and insecurity. Indian parents must overcome these tendencies toward possessiveness and attachment to their children because they create serious obstacles in social, mental, and spiritual life. They should encourage freedom and spontaneity in their children rather than tightly clinging to them. Parents should teach their children to gradually become more and more independent because every child must fly from the nest sooner or later.

In America true culture is lacking because it is a melting pot where people have come from various cultures. The substance in the pot keeps changing, and one does not know what to do in that melting pot. Because America has not yet created its own true culture, family life in America does not have its roots in culture. In addition, technical advancement has created drastic changes in Western family life. The institution of marriage and family life is being ignored. The most vital training ground for the child, the family institution, is disappearing. The American child is insecure because he does not receive the necessary childhood training. A lot of energy and money are being wasted as the courts remain busy with divorce cases, and many psychologists and psychiatrists are occupied in dealing with the problems of marital life. All these problems have come from one root, and that is lack of self-awareness. If one does not know oneself, one cannot communicate with others. This is creating a serious problem in family life and is crumbling American society. On one side America is trying to gain more so-called knowledge through scientific discoveries, while on the other hand the family structure is crumbling because there is no understanding of what it is. How can a culture be created when society does not understand the great values of family life?

When the parents are not able to live harmoniously together, it is chaotic for the children. The extraordinary perception that children have is higher than the knowledge gained by sadhakas who practice yogic disciplines. Adults interact more through speech and thought, but a child communicates through feeling. Feeling is actually higher than the power of thought. Children are very sensitive to their parents' thoughts and feelings because they are very close to them. They are very much affected by the thoughts of their parents and also of other family members and caretakers. It is foolish for parents to think they can let off steam when the children are fast asleep because even during sleep their unconscious records the parents' frustrations, discontent, and arguments. It has been proven experimentally that children in deep sleep are receptive to and affected by the quarrels and disagreements of their parents. These experiments have been done in Germany and in France. During these experiments, once the children had fallen asleep, their parents were instructed to start arguing. While the parents were arguing, the children, instead of creating delta waves, which indicate a state of deep sleep, began to create beta waves, the indication of disturbed sleep. When parents do not love each other and frequently fight and disagree, their words and thoughts definitely have an effect on their children, even during sleep. In such an environment, the children may become restless, have nightmares, and wake up crying. Merely feeding a child to pacify him does not compensate for the disturbance created in the subtle realms of the child's mind.

It is also unhealthy for the parent-child relationship when parents live together on the child's account. Children suffer deeply when their parents are incompatible in married life. The decision of the parents to separate and to divorce creates disaster for the children. I have never seen a child who can be considered normal after the parents have divorced. The tender hearts and minds of children cannot comprehend what has happened. One child said to me, "It suits me." I said, "Why?" He replied, "I live with my mom and I get dollars from my dad. When they lived together, they didn't love me so much. But I don't understand why they do not live together." There is always a conflict like this.

The Western notion of material success also has had a disastrous effect on family life. Modern life, especially in the West, is controlled by the so-called economy, which is not based on needs but on many wants and desires—the sources of extravagance and the dissipation of energy. Competition to obtain more and more external comforts exists at home, among neighbors, and all over the world. For example, how much time, energy, and money do people waste in dressing their skeletons so that they will be accepted by others in this modern society? The desire to be accepted and to be wanted are barriers that inhibit one's growth. It is difficult to know where this competition will ultimately lead humanity. Even in individual families, husbands and wives seem to compete with each other. Adults now place more and more emphasis on success as it is defined in the material world and give priority, not to their children, but to the bills they pay. While holding their children on their laps or sitting next to them, parents discuss their financial successes and failures. This creates feelings of insecurity in the children who look to their parents for strength and guidance. The parents are driven by the pressure to obtain an abundance of material things. Even well-educated mothers feel forced to value material possessions above the duties of raising their child and go out in the world to work. They leave their child either unattended or with babysitters who are strangers. In the turmoil created by the modern world such working mothers naturally feel guilty that their child is not being sufficiently attended to and loved. To compensate they shower the child with the best clothes and the most advanced computer games and amusements. At the same time they create unrealistic expectations that the child must be perfect and must develop according to the current books on child psychology. Rather than being allowed to develop at his own pace and according to his own interests, the child is forced to be the best because he is surrounded by the best in material things. In this way the child himself becomes a thing—just another mechanical toy to be wound up and shown off to company. Contentment remains only a dream and never materializes for such a child.

Parents often want their child to become what they themselves could not be and set goals for the child accordingly. They push the child in a certain direction, whether or not the child is prepared for such goals. Instead of studying the child's behavior and natural inclinations, they force their own ideas onto the child and expect him to fulfill their expectations. This type of parental pressure is heavier than any other. As soon as the child begins to communicate and express himself, parents enthusiastically tell him that he must become a lawyer, or a doctor, or a great scientist. This is ridiculous. It is like a gardener who expects a day lily to bloom like a daffodil. And when he does not see the lily blossom in the daffodil's color, he becomes disappointed and frustrated and fails to appreciate the loveliness of the color of the lily. When the parents' goals are forcibly imposed like this, it creates a great conflict between the parents and the child. The child grows full of resentment, and the fires of discontent burn within. That conflict continues to grow throughout the child's whole life and remains in adulthood. As parents, you should be observent enough to see the child's natural tendencies—the motivations that brought him here. If you study the behavior of the child, you can become aware of these strong motivations. Then you can help him to grow and you can guide him into the world. If parents would study the child's inborn and predominant qualities and inclinations and simply allow the child to grow accordingly, the child would develop more fully. Every human being has potentials. Many of the problems of our society could be solved if parents would help their children to express those potentials in creative ways.

Children need an integrated education rather than a one-sided education that emphasizes only material success. The emphasis on success creates a hurried indigestion in the child's psyche. He is car-pooled here and there all day long—from school to sports, and then to music, art, and dancing lessons. He runs on an adult's treadmill in order to fulfill his parents' dreams, with no free time to exercise his imagination. It is through imagination that children can openly examine their feelings and experiment with the world, and then form their own outlook on life and the external environment. When you interrupt a child's imaginative play and hurry him to dress, bathe, and eat, this robs him of precious moments of learning. No wonder more and more children in the West are being diagnosed as hyperactive and learning disabled. Western children lack serenity because they are mirrors of their parents' anxieties.

Another major problem in Western society is overstimulation. Children are bombarded with stimuli from television, radio, tape recorders, computers, and electronic toys. The producers of children's programs and the manufacturers of games and toys barrage children with wild colors and loud noise devices to capture their fancy. The aim of mass-market production is to convince children to put pressure on their parents to buy as many of these items as possible. Producers and manufacturers rarely pay attention to the developmental needs of children, and parents use little discrimination in selecting their children's television programs and toys. As a result, the Western child's babysitter has become something inanimate and mechanical, with no hugs or words of encouragement. In these circumstances many children become household dictators, ruling what, when, and how they will be entertained. Out of feelings of guilt for not spending more time with their children, the parents often concede. They do not realize that the children are actually asking for loving guidance, not chaotic, free-reign.

Both the modern way and the orthodox way of raising a child seem to be extreme and incomplete. The modern way is mechanical and the orthodox way is rigid. In the modern way of raising a child the mother is told not to make the baby dependent on her; she is encouraged to allow the baby to cry and to

14

leave the baby with a babysitter. This way is equally as dangerous as the orthodox method in which the child must literally follow in the footprints of the parents. The orthodox do not want to accept the child's individuality. Instead they use their child as a means for letting out their frustrations or to fulfill their egotistical way of life. Rather than being loved unconditionally, children are regarded as possessions—pieces of furniture or property—that might fulfill the parents' sense of incompleteness. Some parents are proud to have a child because it satisfies social expectations and feeds their ego. The child's consciousness records all of this, and the child loses something of his or her individuality that can never be recovered by any means.

Although family life is the very basis of society, human beings are still experimenting with the family institution. Human relationships, at peril these days, should not be taken lightly but as something deep and meaningful. Marriage should be seen as a pleasant responsibility and not as a mere game that is played out of biological necessity. Marriage is a process that includes sharing, understanding, and adjusting. Adjustment is a skill that leads to contentment. When two people live together and don't find fulfillment, they start craving for a child. The child becomes a bridge between the two people. When they both work hard and lovingly for the child, they become closer. Married couples should not be irresponsible and bear children if they are not prepared to bring them up wisely and lovingly. It is a very big responsibility to give birth to and to bring up a child. For that responsibility parents should take into consideration more than the selfish motivation of satisfying each other's needs, wants, and urges. Responsibility is not something bad; to take responsibility for something means to learn to give the best that you have. When two people get married not only to satisfy their sexual needs but also to have a child, they should take that responsibility seriously and devote their time to the child so that the child can become a perfect human being. With this understanding and goal in mind, it becomes a great joy and pleasure to bring up a child. If the mother does not understand her duties toward the child, or if the parents are not willing to sacrifice their own pleasures for the sake of the child, the child will still grow but will grow wildly. Such a child will disturb himself and others without understanding the roots of those disturbances.

Sometimes newly wedded couples, even though using contraceptives, discover that they are expecting a child. This becomes a problem for them because they were not yet prepared to have a child. For some time they may consider aborting that child. Later they may decide that the child is theirs and should not be aborted. They are not aware of the *samskaras*—the subtle impressions—that they have been imparting to the child. That child will be born in confusion because the parents were not prepared for it. In today's society parents commonly have communication problems. A child who is brought into the world without any understanding will only contribute to these communication problems.

You should accept the responsibilities of parents from the beginning. If you understand that God has created you as instruments to give birth to someone, it should be a joy for both of you. You should have the attitude that if the Lord wants you to serve someone, you will serve him or her with all your heart and mind. Accept whatever God gives you and learn to love your duties toward your child. Then you will enjoy your child. Birth is not an accident. Parents do not understand this fact and do not prepare themselves to meet and appreciate the uniqueness of the person in their newborn child. When you desire to have a child, first you should ask yourself if you have enough means and if you have the capacity to have a child. More importantly, you should ask yourself if you really deserve to have a child. Not only should you learn how to bring up a child, you should also prepare yourself to deserve a child. This requires a long physical, mental, and spiritual preparation. Some of the child's samskaras come from the behavior, teaching, and understanding of their parents. If the mother is very emotional, the child will also go through that emotional strain. The child of a man who has no control over his temper will also have that weakness.

It is not wise to have a child unless you are fully prepared to raise the child with the understanding that you can also learn from the child, rather than always forcing your ideas onto him. Children want to know things for themselves without any interference and they do not want anything to be forced on them. Your children can teach you many things if you are prepared to learn something from them. From your children you can learn renunciation, charity, and selfless service. Many times you will have to renounce your joys for the sake of your children. For example, you may have plans to go out to a holiday resort but at the last moment you have to cancel because the children are not feeling well. You have to wait for them to come from school; you have to wait for them to go to bed. When you have a child, you will learn to become selfless.

We bank much on the education that is imparted by colleges and universities, but the home is the highest of training grounds. Homes are actually schools for children to learn to play, to love, and to interact with others. At home the different personalities the child encounters help to create the subtle impressions that contribute to building the child's own personality. If the child lives in an atmosphere that is not healthy, how can that child grow properly, become a good citizen, and help others? Parents should provide harmonious homes in which to nurture their children. The home is meant to radiate love selflessly. It is important to respect and revere the ancient institution of the family—for our survival, for the survival of our families, and for the survival of the training ground that is called family life. If we take care of the younger generation, we will find a great change in civilization in our lifetime.

I am not against one culture and in favor of the other but my observation has led me to understand that the modern technological and scientific world should not forget our great ancient cultural values. If the ancient heart is united with the modern mind, this will prevent us from losing what we have and enable us to accept that which is good in the growth of each individual and of humanity as a whole.

CHAPTER TWO

BASIC TRAINING

THE GREATEST TEACHER in India is woman in our family tradition. Our scriptures say: *"Matri devo, pitri devo, acharya devo." Devo* means "bright being."* This saying means that the mother is the first teacher, the father the second, and the spiritual teacher or religious teachings become the third teacher in the child's life. These three teachers provide the child's educational foundation and give the necessary guidance. The mother, from whose loving bosom the first lessons of life are learned, is the first and foremost teacher of the child. If she does not sow the seeds of good conduct and health, the other two teachers will find great difficulty in discharging their duties. It is said that a child starts learning twenty-one years before birth. This means that the mother should be trained before she conceives a child so that she can love and educate her child in a manner that is comfortable and healthy for both.

A woman should actually work hard before having a child if she really wants to have a healthy child. Not only should she strive to improve her physical health, she should also work on herself and try to transform her personality for the sake of her child. When a woman is expecting a child, she should have a very nutritional diet, she should exercise, and she should read inspiring books. Her husband should treat her very nicely. He should respect her, look after her, and should not create any emotional problems for her; he should understand that she needs love and sympathy. The child is affected by the way the mother thinks before and during pregnancy and will have the same tendencies as the mother has. Therefore, when a woman is pregnant she should not think in a negative way, she should not be depressed, and she should not become emotional. The mother's thoughts and behavior affect the child she is carrying because the child's sensitive heart accepts anything and everything.

The education of the child can begin from the first day of pregnancy. You can read an example of this in the Mahabharata, one of the great epics of India. Arjuna was the great warrior of the battle of the Mahabharata. When he would come back from the battlefield, he would discuss the techniques of fighting with his wife, who was pregnant. She was not interested in listening to these things. So he said, "Listen, I am telling you these things to educate our child. Please listen to me. I will tell you the techniques of fighting so that our child learns." She said, "How is it possible?" He said, "Make a note of what I am saying." Then he explained to her the technique of how to build a fort that the enemy could not penetrate. He also wanted to explain how to invade the fort of the enemy but he was not able to complete the lesson because his wife had fallen asleep. At the age of twelve years, their son, Abhimanyu, could describe how to create a fort that the enemy could not destroy. He knew this because of the subtle samskaras he had received when he was in his mother's womb.

Nature has provided a wonderful mechanism for the mother to freely enjoy the company of her child for nine months. She alone can communicate with and feel the child she is carrying. She should realize this is something great and learn to enjoy it. During the months of pregnancy the father does not directly feel the living presence of the child as does the mother. Before the child's birth the father simply feels excitement, curiosity, and pride for his child. Man does not have the power that woman has to carry a child for nine months. If you put a little pebble on a man's abdomen, and tell him to carry it for two or three days, he will not be able to do so. Woman is superior to man; woman has tremendous strength and capacity to go through many pains in life. Man has been irresponsible throughout the ages. The family institution was established by woman. It was woman who felt the necessity of establishing a home and shelter for her child, so woman is actually the first architect. Now, it is woman's responsibility to build our society. That which man has not been able to do, woman should do because she can do it. All women should be aware of the wealth they have. No woman should ever feel she is inferior because she is a woman. Woman has great power and great responsibility. The child's education is totally in the mother's hands. If all mothers would decide to do their duties lovingly toward their children, in one day they could considerably reduce the misery of the world. All mothers should realize that they can change the whole course of their child's life. Although raising a child is a mutual responsibility, most men do not care to know or understand the necessity and importance of loving, caressing, and teaching the child. It is man's nature to be extroverted. It is more difficult for him to be sensitive to the responsibilities of child raising. Usually the man is not helpful to his wife in caring for an infant. Many new fathers feel jealous when the attention once paid to them is suddenly given to the infant. As a result, they frequently stop being nice to their wives and start grumbling for want of attention. The man of the house thus often proves his uselessness and inability in helping to bring up the child, and the mother is the lone lover of her tender infant.

Many great men throughout history have paid tribute to their mothers in gratitude for their good fortune or fame. The call of motherhood is surely the highest, for the mother loves her child unconditionally. A mother is naturally able to beautifully communicate with her infant silently, even though the infant does not understand the thoughts, desires, and whims of the mother. If the baby is crying, and the mother starts coming toward her, the baby becomes quiet. This is called silent communication, the language of love. Even though a mother does everything for her child, she never expects anything in return. She remains busy throughout the day in feeding her child, cleaning her child, and thinking about how her child will grow. A mother is never disappointed, no matter how many silly things the child does. It is her pleasure to look after her child. In return, the child loves his mother because she is constantly serving him. Otherwise the child would know only self-love. If the mother's love is not there, how will the child be able to return love?

Although woman has a natural inclination and instinct to have and to love a baby, a woman who has had no training in the responsibilities of motherhood often commits mistakes that are hurtful to the child, even though she does not consciously intend to do so. If a teacher does not know her subject, how can she teach the student? The parents of a first child are often inexperienced in childcare, and many mothers lack the basic knowledge needed to care for an infant. New parents frequently make errors in the following areas: feeding the child, caring for the child's health, spending enough time with the child, and disciplining the child, while at the same time allowing him to grow according to his own potentials.

Modern parents may not have training in how to feed an infant. Ideally a baby should be breastfed up to the age of about one year. For feeding the baby, the mother should sit up, rather than lie down, and hold the baby in the lap. I have also seen mothers who do not know how to hold a baby after feeding. As a result, gases form and create discomfort, and the child starts to cry. The child needs to expel these gases after feeding and for this should be held upright to the breast. Once I was visiting the parents of a new baby and I observed that after feeding the baby they put her in the crib and started to sing a song. The baby was restless because of the gases that had formed. I said, "Please, hug your baby. You don't hug your baby." They said, "Oh, no. We love our baby." I said, "No. Just lift the baby after she feeds and hug her." After they did this, and the baby had dispelled the gases that had formed, she went to sleep.

Many new mothers also do not know that their own gastric problems may be passed on to the child through breastfeeding, and that they need to be careful with their own diet and the food that they eat while they are breastfeeding the child.

Sometimes parents think they have to feed their baby mechanically after every three hours and even wake the baby at night for feeding. Once when I was staying at somebody's home I noticed that the mother was waking up her two-month-old baby at two o'clock in the morning. "Get up baby, get up. I have to feed you." The poor baby was screaming, and the mother was trying to force-feed her. The next day I asked her, "Who told you to do this?" She replied, "My doctor told me to feed the baby after every three hours." I said, "Did he tell you to disturb the baby when she's fast asleep?" She said, "Maybe I did not understand what he meant." You should allow a baby who is sleeping to wake up of her own accord. It is not good for the health of the baby when you disturb her sleep after every three hours. When the baby is fast asleep, there is no need to wake her up. When she is hungry, she will ask for food by crying. There is no need to create an artificial feeding schedule. The child also knows better than the mother what his capacity is and you should not force him to take more than he wants. Force-feeding, which I call nagging love, can sometimes create a serious problem in the child. After some time he will cry and refuse to drink the milk. Such force-feeding can make a child obstinate and can create in him an aversion to food. An obstinate child will continue to build up resistance and defense mechanisms to isolate himself from others. He will not freely communicate with his parents, teachers, and friends. From the very beginning suspicion, doubt, and lack of confidence will cause him to retreat into his own private world. Such isolation will prevent him from sharing and exchanging with others, and there will be no reciprocity in his behavior. If this habit is not removed in early life, the child will remain in this private world throughout all the stages of his growth and development. In later life these defense mechanisms and the habit of isolating himself will create serious barriers for him, and he will not be able to relate with friends or even with his wife. Incompatibility with one's partner is an outgrowth of habits acquired in childhood. No matter how many therapists, psychologists, psychiatrists, or counselors try to help such a person, it remains hard for him to regain confidence and to relate to his partner. These problems originate in childhood due to innocent mistakes unconsciously made by the parents.

Mothers should also understand that every time a baby cries it's doesn't necessarily mean that the baby is crying for food. There could be another reason: the room temperature may be too hot or too cold; the baby may feel uncomfortable in her position in bed; mosquito bites or itching may be disturbing the baby; or the baby may be having unpleasant dreams. Many mothers are not sensitive to the dreaming habits and nightmares of infants. Infants dream exactly the way others dream. Anyone who experiences the waking state surely dreams. These dreams are caused by the atmosphere and the state of cleanliness of the room in which the child sleeps. Sounds created near the sleeping child also have a profound effect on the child. You can even teach a child who is fast asleep and the conscious mind has calmed down, and send thought forms to a sleeping child for his improvement. However, no agitating sounds should uselessly be created in the room where the child is sleeping. Harsh music, like rock and roll and disco, should not be played near the child. The infant's body may jerk at the sound of thunder or other loud noises. Jerks and tremors of the body during sleep are symptoms of restlessness. When the child is experiencing such disturbances, she should be held in the lap where she will instinctually feel completely secure.

It is also important that the mother adjust to the infant's sleeping patterns. For instance, a new baby usually wakes up many times in twenty-four hours. This may upset the mother's sleeping habits so much that she may become angry and perturbed. Many times a mother, out of anger, may even drop the child onto the bed, an undeserved punishment. Such behavior towards an innocent child creates guilt feelings in the mother, for which she will continue to suffer and punish herself for a long time. When the mother is able to understand and accommodate the infant's sleep cycle, it creates a long-lasting sense of tranquility in the child.

Another source of conflict between mother and child can arise if the child is not allowed to sleep in the same room with the parents. These days there is a theory that the child should not sleep in the parents' room. The doctor tells you not to allow your child to stay in your bedroom because it will disturb your and your husband's sleep and that it is unhealthy for your relationship. Does it seem reasonable to put a newborn baby in a separate, dark room for your personal pleasures? Do you not want to be near your child just because the child disturbs your joys? When a new-born baby is separated from the mother immediately after birth, the closeness between mother and child is disturbed. Many children have emotional problems because of being separated from their mother so soon after birth. What is the harm if the baby remains close to the mother in the same room for some time? Is the relationship of the parents more important than the mother-child relationship? Separating a newborn from the mother is a dangerous thing that is being practiced, particularly in the West. If parents continue this practice, they will never be close to their children, no matter how much they try.

Concerning the child's health, the mother should educate herself in preventive methods and natural health care rather than allowing modern physicians to blast the child's tender system with various drugs and sedatives for every minor ailment. Excessive drugging has adverse affects on the child's sensitive system. All drugs have possible side effects and may specifically affect the nervous system or result in impaired hearing or bad eyesight or they may generally weaken the immune system. The fewer drugs given to the child, the healthier he will be. For at least the first year in the child's life the parents should maintain constant vigilance and keenly observe the child while the child is feeding and sleeping. In the child's first year many illnesses can creep into the child's system due to allergies or sensitivities to substances in the environment and to new foods. It is important not to suppress such allergies with drugs and ointments. To remove these temporary illnesses it is often helpful to change the environment and even the cooking utensils. But if these allergies are not appropriately dealt with in the early stages, they can have a negative impact on the child's mind and body and can even create chronic illness.

I would also like to mention that many mothers forget to give water to their child. Thirst cannot be compensated by milk or any kind of juices or liquids; thirst can be quenched by water only. Boiled water that has been cooled should be given from the very beginning. A child who is not given water may develop constipation, thus causing worry and confusion in the parents. If the family physician or child specialist is not conscientious, she will unnecessarily prescribe laxatives and purgatives for the child.

The start of weaning may be the first time that the child experiences a sense of insecurity. I have observed great confusion during the transition period when the child is being weaned, and food other than mother's milk is introduced to the child for the first time. The child should be weaned in a gradual and gentle manner. During the process of weaning, pacifiers are not healthy or helpful, and new foods should be slowly introduced. When breastfeeding is suddenly and completely stopped, and the child is fed cow's milk or other milk, it can be a shock to the child's system. Many children suffer on account of such an abrupt change.

In the years of growth and development that follow infancy, the child should be given nutritious foods. Mothers should study something about diet and nutrition so they understand the proper way to nourish their child. Nutritious foods should be carefully chosen for the child's meals, and the foods should be simple and fresh. A child's food should not be roasted and toasted overenthusiastically or prepared with too many spices and flavors. Food that has been roasted and toasted too much may be very tasty, but it has no nutritional value. Within the daily schedule mothers should allow enough time to prepare nutritious meals for their children and to serve them in a calm and loving atmosphere. Nutritious foods and nourishing conversation should be the two main ingredients in every meal. Because meat is often considered to be the most important part of the diet, many people give meat to their child before the child is even one year of age. This is not necessary. A child needs nourishing food that he can easily digest and that he can enjoy. Children not only need nutritious food, they should also be taught to understand what to eat and what not to eat. Fast foods have a high sugar content that depletes the body of energy and leads to wide swings in emotional moods.This is particularly true for the child's tender system, but Western parents ignore this fact and often choose the fastest and easiest foods. This is why children in the world's wealthiest countries are starving! Although there is abundant food to eat, the quality of most Western meals does not meet the needs of growing children.

Out of generosity and a sense of loving service, it has been the tendency of Indian women to overfeed their children. Overfeeding is also not healthy for children, despite the good intentions of the mother.

Mothers frequently do not realize the importance of teaching their children to properly chew their food and to brush their teeth after each meal. Both of these practices have a deep impact on a child's health and character. The more one chews, the less one eats; and the less one eats, the better one eats. If a child does not learn how to chew his food properly and to brush his teeth, he will have long-lasting and serious digestive problems.

The atmosphere surrounding the activities of eating, brushing the teeth, going to the bathroom, and preparing for bed should always be peaceful and positive. The imposition of artificial time limits on children creates the parent-child arguments that ring through many Western homes all day long, and especially before bedtime. Children should never go to bed crying and frustrated, feeling as though their parents simply want to get rid of them. Likewise, children should also not feel that going to bed is a punishment. Working mothers and fathers should refresh themselves before the children's bedtime so that they can create a happy transition between the children's waking and sleeping states.

Just as bedtime should be soothing, certain comfortable routines should be followed to bring the child back to wakefulness in the morning. Lazy parents allow their children to sleep too much. The parents should arise early enough to compose and center themselves so that the stage is set for a day of enjoyable activity for the entire family. A child's day should begin peacefully, rather than with an abrupt awakening by the sound of the parents arguing. The day's rhythm is set by the parents' voices and physical movements around the house. Parents who are disorganized create confusion for the child because he does not know what to expect.

Parents should structure the child's day according to the child's individual needs and rhythms and with enough time to play. The child's play should be supervised by the parents. In fact, parents should spend time with their children and teach them many things, such as the names of flowers, and the way mechanical things work; they should tell them stories of heroes and great people, and read to them. It is best to make a daily routine for the child which includes physical exercise and enough time for eating, going to the bathroom, and independent activities so that the child remains happily occupied throughout the day. If the child knows there is some framework to his day, he will naturally fall into that framework and will take responsibility for doing things on time. Time is the greatest of all teachers. If a schedule is made in such a way that the child learns to do things on time, he will not become lazy at a later age.

The first person a child comes to know and understand is the mother because the child is very close to the mother. The mother is the first teacher of the child and if she does not impart the right knowledge to the child, then the child will not really grow or mature well. A mother should be very careful in bringing up her child and should impart those subtle methods and lessons that will help the child to grow. If the mother is calm and intelligent, the child will also have the same qualities. If the mother does not know how to give lovingly and freely to the child, then the child will also be selfish. The overall health of the child is a matter of the mind and heart, good nutrition, and above all, the tender loving care of the mother.

CHAPTER THREE

CHILD DEVELOPMENT

THERE ARE CERTAIN universal themes that dominate the different stages of the child's development. Each of these stages has a distinct purpose and a beauty of its own; each stage of growth unfolds from the previous stage. Parents must learn to recognize these universal themes and encourage the child to experience each stage of development freely. Unless parents understand these stages, they cannot properly guide the child toward adulthood. Education cannot be left entirely to the schoolteachers. The seeds which are sown in early childhood are the real foundation for education. Parents must train themselves so they can become the child's teachers and friends. Let us examine some of the universal themes of childhood that, if properly understood, can help parents design avenues to lead the child to mastery of himself and his world.

During *infancy* the child's primary concern is just to play and he thinks that everything in the world is a toy meant just for him. At this stage it is helpful if you hold the baby gently and talk to him with loving expressions and soothing sounds. Actually it is the child who teaches the mother what his needs are, and there is a very subtle and pleasant exchange between the two. They teach each other all through the child's infancy until the child's consciousness starts to expand.

Although *early childhood* is unabashedly joyous, this is often the most misunderstood period in the child's development. It is during the toddler years that parents and children have to make the greatest adjustment and learn to understand each other's habits, language, and behavior. Children from the ages of two to four years are avidly interested in language, and this is the age of conversation. The child is becoming fluent in language and can talk with her parents about dinosaurs, thunder, dreams, and whatever makes her laugh and cry. She can begin to understand jokes and retell them with sense, and she can feel and sustain a sense of sadness and know why. At this stage the child enjoys spontaneous word games with the emphasis on sound rather than on sense. Parents should join in these word games and understand that they are an important basis for reading and writing, and for developing the child's confidence in self-expression.

Also during this stage children start to master their physical movements that began with crawling and walking and now are advancing to balancing, climbing, and skipping. Gross motor development is the most active from the ages of two to five years, when children love to show off this newly discovered physical self-mastery. Children need to run freely, to climb, and to jump in order to release the excitement they feel just in being alive. Parents often unnecessarily guard their child and do not allow him to crawl freely, to knock down toys, or to build mud houses. Such extravagant protectiveness and overemphasis on cleanliness lead to suppression of the child's creative abilities. Many parents are overcautious and fuss over the child every time the child has a minor fall. This makes the child apprehensive and destroys the sense of self-confidence in the child. Parents should allow their child to be daring, within the limits of common sense, and should not overprotect or overcaution him.

The importance of developing a healthy relationship with one's body at this early age cannot be overemphasized. A child can never learn to quiet himself mentally if he has not learned how and when to express himself physically. It has been proven that a child who does not learn to crawl will later have difficulty learning to read. Such evidence indicates that a child must begin with mastery of the most active layers of his being in order to develop the quieter, more subtle levels. Similarly, a child's fine muscle co-ordination and eye-hand coordination develop from the gross to the subtle. A toddler begins by making gross squeezing movements of his fist and soon is able to use his fingers more delicately in preparation for grasping a pencil. Parents often become impatient with the child's lack of physical coordination so that even a minor event such as spilled milk becomes traumatic. They blame the child for his physical limitations, and this leads to guilt feelings and lack of self-esteem in the child. Psychologists have written much about the danger of a judgmental approach to toilet training. Suffice it to say that any time a parent says, "You are bad;" "You shouldn't;" or "Don't," the child loses a small part of his inborn confidence.

When a mother sees her child fighting, she may often try to justify his behavior and fight his battles for him. This hinders the development of the child's faculty of discrimination. He thinks that because all his actions are approved by his mother, he must always be right. Throughout his life he will continue to search for confirmation and approval of all his actions. When he does not get this approval, he loses confidence, becomes unsure of himself, and is unable to make decisions at the right time and place.

It is during early childhood that the child develops various loves, beginning with love for the breast and the blanket, and expanding to love for toys, dolls, and tiny objects. Three-year-olds go through a stage of orderliness that can be confusing to parents. Parents should realize that this is not obsessive behavior, but a natural attempt by the child to bring order into his world of familiar and loved possessions. Beginning with his attachment to the breast in infancy, the child sees all things as parts of himself, as "mine". As his consciousness expands and he begins to distinguish between himself and others, he learns to understand the difference between "yours" and "mine". Parents often force their children to share toys when they are still too egocentric to understand the meaning of sharing. Egocentricity in children is not equivalent to the adult quality of selfishness, but rather is a stage through which children naturally pass. Compelling a child to share, in fact, has negative effects. The child becomes resistant and does not learn true selfless giving. Initially most children socialize through parallel play. That is, they do not play together in groups, but across from or beside one another, each in his own space and occupied with his own activity. If children's play areas are set up to respect these boundaries until they feel secure enough to share their games and toys with their playmates, there will be peaceful socializing. One of the best introductions to sharing is to have a child prepare and offer food to another child. For example, some nursery schools encourage children to take turns preparing slices of apples and carrots to serve to the other children. Such experiences allow a child to give with pride that which he himself has made. By the age of three years the child begins to discover the excitement of friendship with her peers. By five years she is able to engage in group play, and enjoys making up group games with elementary rules, which she and the group scrupulously enforce.

It is also during the two-to-four-year period that the child develops the desire to control his own environment. As a result, he loves to participate with adults in simple household tasks like washing dishes, polishing shoes, pouring liquids, buttoning and zippering, and measuring and sifting. While these activities may seem insignificant, they help to develop fine motor skills, and teach the child discrimination and the natural consequences of his actions. What better way is there to explore some of the fundamental principles of chemistry and physics than by baking a cake with mother? Hours worth of creative games can be devised from simple household and garden tasks. These activities also allow children to model the behavior of their parents. It is at this stage that the child identifies with his parents and with television and comic book heroes. His mind is absorbent and he mimics the behavior and speech of the adults surrounding him. This presents a challenge for parents because all of their actions—both good and bad—are adopted by their children. Parents should discuss with each other and openly examine their own attitudes and behaviors in a non-judgmental way so that they can agree on a united approach to teaching the child by example.

A child takes in information through the five senses—smelling, tasting, touching, seeing, and hearing. The primary function of the senses is to discriminate between the objects of the external world. A child's senses should be stimulated, but not overstimulated, so that he can learn to harness them. Sensory education teaches the child to distinguish colors, hues, tastes, smells, and textures, and graduations in size and weight, sounds, and tones. Being able to make these distinctions enables the child to use the objects of the world for his own enjoyment. At first the child should be given only a few objects, rather than a confusing array of choices. In this way he can choose for himself and experience feelings of success.

Fear is one of the greatest obstacles to growth. From the very beginning children are taught to be afraid of so many things and they are given so many "don'ts": not to do this, not to go near the fire, not to go near the electrical outlets, not to go near the car— the poor children don't know where to go. Children often develop phobias during early childhood as their imaginations awaken. They live in imaginary fears. Whatever the fear, whether of darkness or ghosts, it springs from imagination and insecurity. A child will continue to create fears for himself throughout his whole life unless he is taught to examine these fears. For example, he should be taken to the dark room of which he is afraid and should be shown that by turning the switch on and off he himself has the power to create darkness, and that darkness holds nothing to harm him.

Dreams can also create fear for children. It is not necessary to take a child who has fearful and upsetting dreams to psychologists and psychiatrists.

Instead, parents should discuss the dreams with the child and explain them to him so that he understands the difference between reality and his imaginary fears. These discussions have a dual purpose: they encourage the child to express his feelings, and they help the parents to understand the source of the child's fear so that the fear can be overcome. When parents understand the child's dreams, they can become more aware of the level and manner of the child's thinking process.

There are some dangers for children that are real. Perhaps the greatest of them is "stranger danger". During his early years the child blindly trusts whoever gives him treats and toys. But when the child begins to explore the world independently, he must be made aware that not all adults are like his family. He should learn to discriminate between strangers and those he knows well enough to trust, without being made afraid of strangers altogether.

Perhaps the most delightful quality of early childhood is the child's ability to forgive. One may say that the child forgives because of his unsophisticated memory and undeveloped sense of cause and effect. But he also forgives because he is trusting, innocent, and loving by nature. Forgiveness is that quality, which if cultivated early, can help a child not to brood on hurts but to be always happy and open to the next experiences. We can learn much from the child's ready smile.

Mothers of children who are four-to-seven-years of age should take time to talk to them about their feelings. Children should be encouraged to express their feelings to someone whom they love, and that person should listen with full attention. When you talk to and listen to a child at this age, it gives her a sense of identity and worth. Whenever the child is unusually serious, parents should talk to her lovingly and try to discover the reason for her pensiveness. The child who is listened to learns to listen; and the child who is allowed to express her feelings verbally will not need to express them through tantrums. Children are very pure-hearted; they only react. If you call them fools, they will also tell you that you are a fool. If you say, "I love you," they will also say, "I love you." There is nothing bad in their minds; they are like pure echoes. Children need free time to play, a place to dig for treasures, a little garden—even if it is just a window box—a pet (if the parents can afford it), materials for scribbling and drawing, and a home where their friends are always welcomed.

It is said that the best way to stunt creative ideas is to laugh at them, to ignore them, or to condemn them. Children should be allowed to think, to know, and to argue. Parents and teachers should learn to provoke children's minds so that they start to think and to know more. That is called pleasant pro-vocation. One should always speak intelligently to children. Gandhi used to spend two hours every day talking with children and he considered those times he spent with children the best hours of his life.

Childhood learning problems often develop because of negligence, ignorance, and lack of attention from the parents and the child's brothers and sisters. Sometimes foolish parents love one child more than they love their other children. They may hug one child and speak against another child, and that is not good. When a child's family members consider him to be an odd duck, he comes to believe that he is not as good as his brothers and sisters. Parents add to this lack of self-esteem when they scold such a child and praise his brothers and sisters. This is actually dangerous for the growth of both the child and his siblings. Uselessly praising a child feeds the child's ego. On the other hand, condemning a child in front of other children again and again creates an inferiority complex in the child's heart and mind.

Similar problems can also come from the child's teachers at school. Sometimes teachers discriminate and dislike certain children. Whenever you feel your child is being unfairly treated in school, it is very important that you go to the school and talk with the teacher. Children are children and should be treated properly. When school-age children have bad dreams and nightmares, they may dream of teachers with frowning faces who scold and even spank them. I have observed a few children who, while dreaming, can recite a poem that was memorized in school and reproduce verbatim dialogues they have had with their parents, teachers, and friends. Actually, these dreams indicate that the child is under a lot of stress.

Although dreaming can be a profound kind of therapy, children should not be encouraged to become dreamers. There is another kind of dreaming that we call fantasizing or daydreaming. Whenever children fantasize or their talk becomes influenced by hallucinations, parents should explain the difference between what is real and what is merely pretend. If this is not done, the child will become dull and retreat into a fantasy world, instead of being bright, cheerful, and alert. Such a child will never become a practical, levelheaded person. Children live in a unique world and create a reality of their own. If that reality coincides with the factual world, they make immense progress. But if they lose touch with the objective world, they remain in their own reality and develop communication problems that hinder their progress. A child who is unable to communicate, even though he may have a healthy body and a good education, will not be able to effectively communicate later on in adulthood. First, children need to relate to the facts of the objective world. This gives them a profound base upon which to build their imagination. Fantasies that are unrelated to reality, and hallucinations, are not healthy for the growth of the child. I have seen many children who, because they indulge in such fantasies, become introverted and unable to communicate in a coordinated and realistic way, either with adults or with other children. When such a child is mocked by other children, he starts to compare himself to the other children and wonders what is wrong with himself. This creates an inferiority complex and a serious guilt problem in the child's heart and mind.

As the child matures, adults may depend on him to take care of little brothers and sisters, to get things for the adults' comforts, and to give up playtime to do busy little tasks. This only builds resentment in the child's heart. Childhood ends prematurely for children who are forced to become too responsible at an early age. Children are little persons who come to us as guests. They are not servants or extensions of their parents' egos. They should be taught how to adjust to the family first, and later to society.

Along with the virtues developed in childhood, the child also can acquire certain bad habits that create serious barriers to his growth. The most dangerous period is between seven and fourteen years when the child can develop habits of disrespect, such as foul language, name-calling, ridicule, and self-abuse. These habits may also include fibbing, cheating, stealing, masturbating, or engaging in homosexual activity. Such habits should not be considered to be normal. The ill effects of such bad habits should be explained to the child, or they may well continue to the last breath of his life. Children naturally experiment with many types of behavior. But they should be taught not to do things that form deep habits or that are injurious to their mental and physical health. Both girls and boys can become victims of the mysterious, premature, and harmful urge of masturbation, which arouses undue curiosity and prompts the search for a friend or companion with whom to share this phenomenon. Many psychologists in the Western hemisphere consider these habits to be harmless, but they are mistaken. Such immature opinions are part of the yet to be developed psychology of the West. A time comes when girls and boys begin to keep secrets and stop talking freely to their parents. Many parents do not talk to their children about sexual feelings. In the East such talks are prohibited because of society's taboos. However, if the sexual urge remains always suppressed, when the child becomes an adult, these suppressions will dominate his life. Suppressions come forward in later life in many ways—as illnesses, obsessions, complexes, or stammering. Part of Freud's theory of sexuality is accurate. The child's search for sexual identity is a large part of his personality. That is, a child feels a difference between himself or herself and children of the opposite sex. Boys do not want to be thought of as girls, or girls as boys. Children's desire for sexual identity and acceptance means that they unconsciously understand their difference, and this difference is the basis for sexual feelings. In my opinion at least one of the parents should have a good enough friendship with the child so that he or she can explain love and sexuality to the child. This should be done in a mild, gentle, and loving manner through inspiring stories of great people, and stories that help the child to understand that certain habits are injurious to him. The child should never be told that any of his feelings are bad or should not be experienced. Parents must do everything they can to encourage the child not to be shy, but to freely communicate everything that he or she feels. In modern society there is a preoccupation with sexuality and a pressure for children to be sexually aware at an early age. Thus a pattern develops that has an element of sexual play and sexual talk with flirtatious behavior and increasing tension. This excitement jars and agitates a child's nervous system and becomes associated with the individuals whose thoughts, speech, and deeds have aroused these reactions. But children do not yet have the maturity to handle the feelings and tensions created by this sexual pressure from society.

Both the pattern of suppressing emotions and that of expressing emotions without understanding their nature create great confusion in children. Children in the modern world need education that helps them to understand their sexuality and the changes they are experiencing. They should also be taught what is injurious and what is not. In order to help young people, adults should be aware that children are exposed to certain values through the media and through television programs, and they should examine and scrutinize the media and television programs their children watch. Children are constantly bombarded by these stimuli and they are unable to cope adequately with this agitation and arousal. Constant, friendly guidance is essential for children, especially during puberty. Children should be taught to sublimate and channel their desires through socially accepted substitutes so that they don't experience the many deep frustrations that seem to be personal in the beginning but later become related to others.

The best and most important period of life is childhood, and if the right seeds are sown in childhood, one truly grows and develops.

CHAPTER FOUR

EDUCATION

THE PURPOSE OF EDUCATION is not only enlightenment and salvation, but also to teach one how to conduct oneself in society. Childhood is the best time for real education or basic education. I am not talking about the education that comes from school and the study of books and the memorization of poems; I am referring to the education that comes from the environment. Children learn through observing their environment and the behavior of the people around them and then they naturally imitate what they have observed. This is called education by example. A child's real education is at home, and the first teachers of the child are the mother and the father. Therefore it is very important that parents create the proper environment at home. When the home environment is unstable, and the persons around them are confused and depressed, children cannot get a proper environmental education.

Parents commit two serious mistakes in bringing up children. The first is that they try to teach their children to imitate them. They tell them, "You should imitate me and do exactly as I am doing. If I walk like this, you should also walk the same way; if I talk like this, you should talk like this." Parents teach such things in the name of mannerisms or etiquette. This is not eduation but merely imitation. To tell a child to do something is not the best way. It is the nature of children to imitate. A child will imitate her mother, just as her mother imitated her own mother in her childhood. Most children pick up the accent of their teachers and parents because they naturally imitate.

When it comes to training children, there is nothing like Western children or Eastern children. Children are children and they need good examples to follow. Unfortunately, parents today do not stand as examples. This is the second mistake parents make. In these modern times parents do not impart the main responsibilities of a human being to their children. If children by nature are born selfish, how can the parents help them? The parents will have to demonstrate selflessness so that the children will learn that selflessness from them. But if the parents are selfish, how will the children learn selflessness? Those who want to have children, and those who are already parents, should learn to live selflessly so they are giving the right example to their children. In turn the children will be able to impart the same knowledge to their own children. Parents should understand that selflessness is an expression of love, and they should be very careful in their behavior with their children so that the children have that burning example. The children will naturally imitate and follow the good example of their parents. This is very important. When parents become a good example for their children, they will imitate that example and will grow in happiness, without fear or selfishness.

When a child reaches school age, parents abdicate their roles as teachers and leave education to the institutions. If the child's parents have not completed their duties, then the teachers at school will have difficulty. By this time the child may have become very stubborn and may refuse to accept things as they are. He wants to accept things only if they are as he wants them to be. This creates a very serious obstacle to learning, and it becomes very hard for the teachers to deal with such a child's negative thoughts and habit patterns.

Formal education should expand all of the child's experiences and bring him into contact with a wider circle of loving adults. However, most parents and teachers do not work together to formulate a system of education to fulfill that goal. Instead, parents and teachers either ignore each other or remain at odds throughout the child's formal education. This sort of conflict in the adult world surrounding the child leads to confusion of values in the child's mind. Whom should he believe—his parents or his teachers? Whom should he accept as the authority? It is confusing to a child's mind to live with one set of rules at school and another set at home.

Actually, what we call education is basically nothing but memorization. When children go to school and are exposed to such education, how can they grow properly? Modern education creates merely a superficial coating on the conscious mind. The focus of modern education is on memorizing facts of the external world; it ignores the growth and development of the inner being. Such education creates internal conflict and often, a serious barrier to the faculty of discrimination. It thus hinders the child's ability to make decisions and blocks the progress of the child's growth.

Modern education in both the East and the West shares the same tragic flaw; education helps one to understand and to be successful in the external world, the world of means. It doesn't help one to know oneself. It presents only the means to stimulate the child's external life and fails to explore the child's inner library of knowledge. Thus the child is given the impression that anything that comes from within himself is not valuable, and that the key to all of life's questions comes from the external world. He becomes dependent on other people's thoughts and creativity, rather than developing his own inner kingdom of unique creativity and imagination. The real purpose of education is self-mastery of one's physical, emotional, and mental levels. But today, educators and parents treat the mind as a mere collecting agent or computerized storehouse of unrelated facts that are never directly experienced by the child.

From the very beginning our mistakes are pointed out to us. When we go to school, there also the teacher keeps saying to us, "This is wrong, this is wrong, and this is wrong." The teacher forgets to point out what we may have done correctly. In this way we learn that we make mistakes. When we are brought up in so much negativity, we naturally apply the same thing and form the habit of thinking negatively. We constantly repeat to the conscious mind: *I am full of mistakes, I am hopeless, I cannot do anything.* In school my teachers always used to correct my mistakes, but they rarely pointed out that I had done something good or had written something good. When a teacher corrects a student's mistakes, she could also tell the student, "Look, this is a good thing. Your writing is good and your punctuation is good. You are wonderful; you are really a good student. Now come on." Children do not receive that sort of education. Everybody is prepared to correct their mistakes, but nobody tells them about their good qualities. On the other hand, teachers and parents should also be cautious not to make the child dependent on them for praise and approval.

Teaching is a skill that cannot be taught by any training program. Discipline is an important part of education, but teachers are too often influenced by their own authoritarianism and egotism. Some teachers let out their frustrations on their students in the classroom and impose their authority in an overly rigid way. Teachers should never forget that children learn through love, rather than by rigid disciplines imposed on them. A teacher can be a positive influence by being kind and by being an example, not by beating or forcing the child. When the teacher becomes an example for the students, only then will they naturally start to learn. The teacher should prepare stimulating lessons that provide hands-on experience and then observe and verify the child's experience, just as a scientist verifies the results of an experiment. After having given a simple, clear demonstration of what is to be done, the teacher should then remain silent so that the experience remains the child's alone.

The concept of boarding schools used to be alien to the Indian culture. It was adopted from the British educational system. Even today in India some children are still sent to boarding schools. This type of educational experience has good and bad aspects, but a child should never be sent away from home for schooling before the age of ten. If a child does attend boarding school, the teachers there should continue to observe all of his habit patterns attentively and be able to give him individual guidance as needed.

Not all children develop at the same pace, but parents and teachers expect them to grow in a uniform way. From the ages of five to seven years, children start to show signs of being unable to cope with the pressure to conform. Unfortunately, those children who are unable to keep up with their peers are often mislabeled as slow learners. Actually, except for those few children who suffer from mental disabilities due to a brain injury or a congenital defect, many of these children are not slow at all. When we introduce a curriculum that does not suit the needs of such children, we perceive them as being unintelligent and as failures, whereas actually it is the educational system that is failing the child. The educational system in India has not developed an adequate method for teaching children with learning problems. Such children are simply looked upon as inferior to their peers. This is not a fair attitude because each child has talents of his own; no two children share the same talents and abilities. There are many other ways for these children to develop their skills and to express themselves in a creative way. Parents and teachers should study each child's individual talents and help him to develop his own special gifts. They should understand that many children can accomplish more with their hands than with academic studies.

Actually, there is chaos all over the world in the educational system. The so-called education that is imparted in the world inspires one's ego and leads one on an ego trip. This may be helpful in the external world, but it does not lead to internal fulfillment and satisfaction. We have to learn to organize our society and impart that education which is vital, organic, and very practical. This is not one individual's task; this is not the task of one race, one country, or one nation;

this is the task of the whole of humanity. When we are awakened and we become aware of the existence of others, then we will start doing that. We have not yet attained that state.

In India in ancient times children were taught in *gurukulas,* and spiritual education was a very important part of the curriculum. In the gurukulas the teacher and student's relationship was more than that of parent and child. The teacher always considered a student to be even more than a son or daughter. In modern schools this feeling is absent, and only a technical approach to education is used. Today children may learn facts, but they lose the sensitivity to express their feelings and ideas. Expression is the practical application of facts, a skill that the child needs for the future. The profound type of discipline used in the gurukulas involved all the daily activities of a child during a twenty-four-hour period: How to sit, how to walk, and how to talk; how to be strong and protect oneself; and how to be loving. These practical lessons have been lost in the modern methods of early education.

We cannot go back to the past, but we should not forget the good points of education as given by the ancients. At the same time we must not lose touch with our modern inventions and discoveries. The gurukula system of ancient times may not be practical in today's world, but a more holistic approach to education can be adopted. Such an approach emphasizes spiritual growth along with the development of the intellectual aspects of the mind, and also includes guidance in how to maintain the fitness and health of the physical body. Our educational system should be a mixture of ancient methods and modern information.

Education is very important. Children need good examples to follow, but they don't find such examples. That is why they have difficulty in school. Children need guidance. A child grows with environmental education, the education imparted at home, which you call culture, and the education imparted by the colleges and the universities.

Childhood is something great. In childhood the mind is pure, tender, and receptive. If we impart good education to our children, become selfless examples for them, and give them love, perhaps they will grow and become the best citizens of the world. Then, the whole universe will bloom like a flower.

Chapter Five

Discipline

IF CHILDREN TODAY are wild, it is not because of their own mistakes, but because they have not been given proper love and care; they have not been taught by example. The problems which we see in the younger generation today have come from us. Their emotional problems are not their emotional problems; they are our emotional problems.

Parents create emotional problems in their children because children learn through imitation. They learn from their parents and receive their thought forms; they imitate how their parents behave, talk, and think. Instead of teaching their children, parents give them their problems. As parents, you should sacrifice for your children and give more time to them so that instead of growing wildly they find some interest in life. You look after your children because you think they are your possessions, not because they are good children. You say, "You are my child. You have to listen to me and obey me." This concept should be changed. Otherwise you will find that the family system will slowly fall apart, and it will take a long time to reconstruct it again. They are your children and they need your help and support. You cannot teach children by will; you can teach them by example. They need example and they need love. Unfortunately they don't get these two things. When parents remain selfishly busy in their own affairs and ignore their children, the children inevitably suffer.

In the West children are allowed to grow like little weeds without discipline. Though they are provided with many material things—fine clothes, a room filled with toys, and many modern amenities—the parents do not have time to attend to them. From the very beginning even the best of parents leave their children with a babysitter. Both parents think they have to work because their lives are controlled by the modern economy. Even if the mother is free, she remains busy with her hobbies and her shopping. It is a trend of the modern mind to leave the children with babysitters, and mothers think they are doing a superb job of raising their children when they do so. The parents are so busy that they don't have time for their children. They give everything to their children but love. As a result, when the children grow older, they kick their parents. I am talking to you like this because I have studied these things so deeply. My heart is with the younger generation. When I find them rebellious and wild, I don't blame them. If children do not believe in discipline, it is because there is no example of discipline in their lives. The wisdom that is helpful for the growth and unfoldment of the child is missing; the experience and knowledge that parents should impart is not there. Children know that their parents are wise and more experienced, but the parents do not know how to impart their wisdom to them. Consequently, the children do not communicate with their parents and they do not revere their parents. Some children become very self-centered and don't want to hear anything from their parents or from anyone else. They say they are afraid of talking to their parents because they are very much afraid of being hurt; they say they are afraid of all who are in authority. They become very obstinate and don't want to listen to anyone; they want to experience everything for themselves. When they start to experience in this way, they may go through many serious problems. Sometimes they become victims of certain things that they are never able to come out of throughout their whole life.

On the other hand, parents expect too much from their children and complain that their children do not communicate with them. They put all the blame for the lack of communication on the younger generation. But something has happened to the older generation. The father intellectualizes everything and cannot bring himself down to a child's level; thus he cannot communicate with his children. The mother remains in a state of emotions; she thinks that her children should do whatever she wants them to do. I have seen many women let out their frustrations on their children. The day the mother has fought with her husband, the children will get a scolding or spanking. This happens with the father also. Parents project their personal problems onto their children. When the children say they are hungry, the mother says, "You shut up! I fed you just now. Your father is never nice to me, why should I be nice to you?" This happens so often in our society.

Many mothers think that their children cannot be trained. This is not true. All children can be trained. Any mother who is a little intelligent can easily understand her child, and the child can be trained. In the animal kingdom a horse that has not been disciplined will run here and there in a very disorderly manner. That same horse, if properly trained, will run as guided on the road. The same power or force that goes toward distraction can be regulated and directed toward the right direction. Parents who do not understand this will not know how to deal with their children's behavior.

The teachings imposed in childhood are ridiculous and continue to ridicule us throughout life. From the very beginning repressions and suppressions are there. The word which is most often repeated by parents is *don't*. A life full of "don'ts" strengthens fear and is a prime enemy to human growth. When children are not allowed to play or do things creatively as they want to, the curiosity of the child, which is the very tool for learning, dies. Children should not be constantly told, "Don't do this," and "Do this." Children should be allowed to grow freely, to know, to feel, and to understand. Crying, smiling, and laughing are the most common expressions of children. Children who are not allowed to express their emotions—to weep or to laugh or to enjoy—do not grow properly. When children have stunted growth, there is definitely something happening that their parents do not understand. Parents should always look for the defects in themselves, rather than in their children.

The home should be a loving training center in which children are allowed to be spontaneous, to devise mischievous pranks, and even to shout at the top of their voices unhesitatingly. Then they will be able to reach the heights of creative imagination. But if a child's creative imagination is suppressed from the very beginning, how can he grow? A child without imagination is no more than a department store mannequin—well dressed, but lifeless. Such puppets do not contribute anything creative to society. When creative spontaneity is killed, human beings become mere duplicates of one another. Rather than thinking for themselves, they just do what others do.

Instead of creating a free and pleasant environment, parents frequently spank their child out of anger. They tell him not to do this or that, and if he does not listen to them, they scold him and spank him. Because the child often doesn't even know why he is being scolded, he becomes confused and grows with many conflicts. Simmering scoldings only create fear and guilt and hinder the child's communication with parents and friends. The fearful dreams and nightmares of children are evidence of such a way of life. Fear always invites danger; it robs inner strength and violates the law of human dignity. Guilt is an evil that is a stumbling block in the growth of a child. Children full of guilt are timid and weak and are unable to behave in a free, straightforward way. Children who are not straightforward will tell lies out of fear. One forms such injurious and long-lasting habits in childhood.

Parents frequently complain that their children are destructive, but I see it differently. If in their experiments they break a costly antique, it doesn't matter. They do not see the value in adult's so-called treasures. If they break something, it does not mean they are destructive. The tendencies of children are carelessly joyous, and they should never be treated cruelly or harshly. The first five to seven years of a child's life are the most tender and the most important. During that time especially, parents should never be harsh or rigid with the child. Excessive rigidity ignores the fact that each child has his or her own personality. Rigidity creates boredom, resentment, and rebelliousness in the child. Harsh treatment, excessive criticism, rudeness, and frequent punishments can all damage a child's personality. It is also harmful to children, though unintentional, when parents frequently nag them.

Never spank your child and never be rude to your child. When a child is spanked, he may stop his objectional behavior, but resentment will grow inside, and he may even really become destructive. You should never use physical force or violence on children. If you do not want your children to hit or strike others, why should you strike or slap them? Violence means that you have no self-discipline or self-control. When parents express their emotions without self-control, their children also do not learn to control their emotions or to use their emotional power positively. When you allow your children to annoy you, you are exhibiting your weakness.

A child is a great teacher. That which you cannot learn from your teachers, from others, or from churches or temples, you can learn from a child. Your children are trying to teach you: "Come on mom; don't be weak; be patient with us. Learn to handle the situation." You are not learning to handle it and so you are not doing your duty properly. It is easy to lose your temper and shout at your children, but it is better to talk to them and help them to understand why certain behaviors are wrong. If instead of punishing the child the parents would engage him in conversation and make him understand their objections, perhaps he might stop destroying valuable things at home. Parents should also take the time to listen to their children and should respect their ideas, opinions, and attitudes.

The commandment, "Speak the truth," is a common source of conflict in the disciplining of children. Adults force this injunction on children without ever teaching them what truth is or how to speak truthfully. The father says, "It's very late. Let us all go to sleep." And when they think the children are asleep, the parents quietly slip out and go to the movies. This happened when I was staying with an officer in Delhi. He said, "Swami, the children are asleep. They are quite grownup now and they won't trouble anyone. You are here so we'll go out to see a movie. They should not know it." I said, "I assure you that I won't tell them. But this is not the right way." Actually, the children were only pretending to be sound asleep, and the moment that officer and his wife left, they got up and said, "Let us shout at the top of our voices." I said, "Why?" They said, "Those rascals. When they drink, they shout. But when we want to play, they don't allow us to shout and they spank us if we do. They lie to us. We want to shout. Please help us." So I took them to the roof and they started to shout. I also began to shout with them. The whole neighborhood was amazed. Many officers gathered around the house and saw that a swami was standing on the roof shouting with four children at ten o'clock at night. Someone said, "What has happened? Hey, who are you?" I said, "Look, I am playing with the children. Why do you not play with your children? What do you see in a movie? You go to enjoy shouting, screaming, and laughing. That's what we are doing here."

No matter how much you lie, you don't want your children to lie. So you tell them, "Don't lie, or we will spank you." But children are very sensitive and keenly observe the behavior of their parents. They know that their parents often tell lies. They observe that Mommy is constantly lying to Daddy, and Daddy also lies to Mommy. They wonder why it is all right for their parents to lie, yet they are not allowed to lie. For example, a father who is a busy lawyer may not want to talk to his client on the telephone so he says to his child, "Tell the gentleman that I am not at home." The child is totally confused and says, "But Papa, you are at home. Why are you lying? You spank me when I lie. Why do you do that?" This creates a serious problem in the child's mind and heart, and after some time he begins to lose respect for his parents. A child's first experiments are with his parents, to see their reactions. After having heard his parents repeatedly lie, the child will naturally also start to tell lies. For example, the child who is not good at his studies or has an aversion to his studies and does not want to go to school may lie and say, "I am not well. I have a stomach ache so I am not going to school today." The child who repeats such pretenses develops the habit of trying to escape from reality. This habit of escape only reinforces the aversion to his studies and leads to the accumulation of more guilt feelings in his mind. When he does attend school, he is always afraid because he has not done his homework and is behind in his studies. This is what is happening in your families. There would be no such repercussions from the habit of lying if parents themselves would speak truthfully before their children. In day-to-day life no matter how many lies you tell, you spank your children when they lie and you tell them to speak the truth. But you never give them any example of *how* to practice speaking the truth.

I have not learned a single thing that I did not learn in my childhood: Be kind, be gentle, be strong, be loving and giving, and be truthful. We all learned these things in our childhood. My mother and your mother taught the same principles. We know the principles, but no one taught us how to practice them. That is why the human personality is full of conflicts. Everyone says to speak the truth, and yet no one gives an example of how to be truthful or shows how to practice being truthful. As a result we grow with confusion. We want to be truthful but we do not know what truth is; and we want to be loving but we do not know what love is. When parents do not practice what they teach, children don't find the right example to follow. This is a very serious problem. Not only does it create conflict and confusion in a child's mind, it also results in a breach of trust between parents and child. When children are not given the right example, they grow with mistrust of their parents. Parents should be very careful in their behavior so they are good examples for their children. When parents are very honest with their children, the children also will not develop the habit of lying. However, when children observe that their parents are very selfish and that they are not honest with them, the children will start doing the same things. And the parents will reap the fruits of their karmas for a long time. Parents should not create conflicts in their children's minds. They should learn to sacrifice their own joys and share with their children, rather than being selfish. Otherwise these conflicts will continue to grow in the children's minds and create many other conflicts.

In my childhood I also became very confused. My master never spanked me, but others spanked me and said, "Hey, speak the truth." I was just a kid and I said, "Tell me, what is that truth?" So one day I said to my master, "Teach me. I know that I should speak truth but I don't know how. Will you teach me how to speak truth?" He replied, "The simplest way to speak truth is by not lying. If you do not lie, you are speaking truth. But if you say you are speaking truth and you do not know what truth is, you are just making up your own truth. That is confusion, not truth. Simply do not lie. By not lying you are speaking truth. Do not do what is not to be done according to your conscience. By not doing what is not to be done, you will start to do what is right." My master taught me not to tell people to speak truth nor to claim that I am speaking truth. The simplest way is not to lie. Yoga science says you are constantly blasting and hurting your inner being by lying. When you are afraid, you lie. Don't do that. By speaking lies you don't hurt others, but you hurt yourself. Let your conscience be your witness. When you start to practice, you will find that speaking truth and doing truthful actions will make you strong, healthy, and great—someone who can stand as an example in the family. Parents who are careful in their speech and take all possible precautions against talking nonsense around their children, find that the children also become straightforward and honest.

A child is a living temple. Children should be loved, adored, and trained. That is the great duty of a mother. Children are curious and want to understand the world. Loving parents should learn to channel this curiosity, rather than hindering or suppressing it. Good discipline is not damaging to the growth of a child, but you should not rigidly impose discipline. To discipline a child actually means to help the child to do things on time and to develop good habits. If you want to teach your children such self-discipline, give them gentle and loving attention. If you really love your children and you tell them, "Sonny, don't do that," they will never do it. But if you bribe them with a biscuit and say, "Look, I will give you a biscuit if you don't do that," they will learn to accept bribes, and later on there will be disaster in their lives.

Although crying is usually interpreted as a sign of pain, sometimes a child will cry just to get what he wants. This is a useless and unhealthy habit that only develops weakness in the child. Parents should not give the child everything he wants or bribe him with toys and make promises they cannot keep in order to pacify him. Rather they should determine what the child's real needs are and generously satisfy those needs. If parents explain that talking is better than crying, the child will not need to communicate his desires through tears.

Children need to learn self-respect, self-confidence, and self-discipline. You can help them to learn these things if, first of all, you help them to feel loved and accepted. When children know they are loved, they can easily be taught to be self-disciplined.

As children become older, they need more firmness and a different type of discipline. They should be encouraged to become independent, strong, and self-confident. When parents teach children to appreciate themselves and to find strength and self-confidence within, they are helping them to avoid the temptations of the modern world, such as the use of drugs. If you want to help your children to avoid drugs, love your children and help them to become strong. A time will come when they will understand that you really love them, and that you have good intentions and want them to grow. Then they will know what to do when confronted with the temptations of the world.

Children should always be treated with respect and affection. The whole essence of discipline is wrapped inside a small thing called love.

CHAPTER SIX

LOVE

PARENTS HAVE ONE universal desire—to see their children happy. But we have not as yet found a definition of happiness, neither for the parents nor for the children. The language of childhood is profoundly simple and full of meaningful silence. All children speak the same language—the language of curiosity and uninhibited love. Parents in both the East and the West have forgotten that language. They are too busy to listen, too preoccupied with their own comforts, and too bound by society's traditions to become fluent in the child's tongue. But a child can only be happy if he can express his innermost language, and his parents are his first audience. When the parents are not close to their children, the children will not love and respect them.

True love is absent in many homes today, and often, that which is considered to be love is actually attachment. Attachment blindfolds one and obscures reality. Attachment is not love, for love is always selfless and unconditional. Husband and wife may love each other for many reasons: physical attraction, psychological compatibility, or, most often, because of feelings of insecurity and incompleteness developed in their own childhood. But parents need to develop relationships based on true love so they can share that love with their children.

Tender loving care should be the first step in the education of the child. When children are given care and love, they will definitely be self-disciplined, and they will return that love. If selfless love is freely given to children, they will respond spontaneously with love. Adults underestimate the ability of children to understand and respond to love. If you really love your children, the first step that you will have to take is to teach them through your example, not through your words. Parents think that unless they tell their children something, they will not understand. That is false. The best method of communication is not through the mind or through speech; the best communication is through the heart. Newborn babies instantaneously and silently communicate with their mother through the language of love—the most ancient language and the mother of all languages. When your children speak to you, the older ones will call you father and mother; but your infant, who does not yet know how to express herself through verbal language, uses only monosyllables—ma, ma, da, da. Who do you love more? It is not the older children whom you love more, but the infant in whose expression there is pure love. Love is higher than intelligence. It is love that a child needs most, and that love should be completely selfless, not based on the idea that the child is your possession. You should love your child, not because it is your duty, but because you recognize that your child is a human being who has the capacity to do many things in life and to become someone great in the world. You should play your role and do the best you can for your child by acknowledging the child's individual personality, and by creating a gentle, accepting, and loving environment that will encourage the child's growth. To be able to do that, you need some training.

Many of you were not taught or trained to give, and for this reason you are not able to communicate well with others or trust others. In modern life you have learned to live only for yourself and to use the things that you have, or want to acquire, for yourself. This idea that you live only for yourself is just one concept. There is an entirely different way to live in which you understand that you are meant for others, and you want to serve others and live for others. One concept contracts your personality; the other expands it. When you are selfish, you create boundaries around yourself and live in a self-created, imaginary fortress. When you become selfless, you expand your personality and no longer think only of yourself. Selfless and loving care from the parents is essential to children.

Today people are very much afraid of the word *responsibility*. If you want to develop spiritually, you should never be afraid of the concept of responsibility. Those who are irresponsible are actually very selfish, and selfish people tend to become more irresponsible. But the more selfless you become, the more you will find yourself with a kind of freedom that cannot be imagined by your mere mind. *Responsibility* actually means giving—the ability to respond. It is something one should learn as a child. Initially, children are very selfish by nature; they don't have awareness of the existence of others. But when they are taught to give from the very beginning, giving becomes a part of their life and they feel joy in giving. When a child learns to love and to give, and finds delight in giving without expectation, such a child in later life can lead society.

The most ancient traveler in the world is human love. If you study the history of love, you will come to know and you will understand how human love shifts from one object to another. When a child is born, he first loves his mother's bosom. Slowly that love moves toward toys and sandcastles that the child builds. The child is equally hurt if you destroy those sandcastles as you are if someone destroys anything of yours. As the child grows, that love moves to girlfriends or boyfriends. Later, love shifts to degrees and honors from universities, after which it grows for prestige, position, and the desire to own something to satisfy the ego. That love grows again for a woman or a man, for marriage, and for a home and children. Finally, one wants to find out what love really means. Sometimes those who have lived life very sincerely sit down and laugh. "Honey, what is that love? Are we really satisfied? Yes. We are satisfied with our relationship, but we have not really known what love means." This indicates that although you may have done your duties as a good wife toward your husband, or as a good husband toward your wife; and as a good father and mother toward your children, you have not yet learned to really love. That is why you are still hungry; you are still not satisfied and you still feel that you have to gain something. Why? What is missing is an understanding of the purpose of life. The ancients used to teach their children everyday before going to bed, "I am strong; I am not afraid of anything, because I love all and exclude none. The purpose of my life is to serve others, to help others, and to love others." If children today were to grow up in such an environment, they could become great people who would serve society and stand as examples for society.

We do not know what love is, even though we use this word in daily life. A child can teach you what love is. The first love of a child grows with the follies of selfishness. Initially, he is interested only in his own welfare and comforts. When his comforts and interests are fulfilled by his parents, then he starts getting attached to his parents. In the early years children are selfish, exactly like animals. As animals do not care for other animals but want to eat first, so is the case with children. Their love is self-love, and for that they love their parents. Slowly that love expands, and they start to have consideration for their parents, for their schoolmates and friends, for their neighbors, and for their environment. But from the very beginning they are self-centered, and if they are not trained to give, this deep-rooted attitude will remain with them their whole life. It is always good for parents to teach their children to give to other members of the family at home.

I was given a very important lesson of sharing when I was sixteen years of age. One day I was just getting ready to eat my lunch in our cave in the Himalayas. We used to take only one meal every day so I was very hungry. Suddenly a swami from the mountains came and he also was very hungry. My master said to me, "Leave your food for him." I said, "I am not going to leave my food for him. I am hungry." He said, "Look, you will feel more enjoyment if you give your food to this swami." I said, "You know that I am hungry and that I cannot cook any more food." I was not allowed to cook food during those days because I was expected to just attend to my meditation and to do sadhana. He said, "Just give it and you will feel great joy." I said, "I am finding great difficulty in giving it. How can I know that I will feel great joy after I have given it?" He said, "Just give it. Perform this act of giving. First give him water to wash his hands and feet, and then tell him, 'Please take your lunch.' You have to do it. This is an experiment." After having eaten, that swami said, "I was very hungry. Thank you very much. I am very grateful to you. God bless you." And I felt great joy. You should experiment at home and learn to give. This is the first principle in life.

There is one serious defect in the manner in which you perform your duties for your families. You do things out of sheer habit, thinking that you are doing your duties. But then those duties become a burden on you and you cannot enjoy performing them. When you do your duties in the external world, learn to do them with love. In the ladder of love the first rung is called reverence for your partner. If you do not have respect for your beloved, you cannot love that person. In Sanskrit this is called *bhakti*. Bhakti is a mixture of two words—love and devotion. If you have love for your family and you are devoted to your family, you will enjoy your duties. Otherwise you will only be working like slaves.

Children need love and care, but modern attitudes of upbringing are turning children into monsters. You say you love your children, but often that is not true. Many children are emotionally and/or physically neglected and abused today. Sometimes parents take out their negative emotions on their children and beat them. Some mothers spank their young babies when they cry. The baby then develops a habit of crying for the mother's love and attention. This is often the first habit a baby learns unconsciously. This habit becomes part of the unconscious and part of the child's personality, and the poor child grows up expecting attention all the time from his relationships. A life full of expectations creates dependency, which is like an addiction. This addiction disorganizes the inner frame of life; it is more dangerous than alcoholism and drug addiction.

Between childhood and adulthood there is often a period of rebelliousness during which children want to express themselves with all their might but cannot do so because of the barriers that were created for them in childhood. Children want to enjoy all they can experimentally and experientially. They go forward in search of the joys of the external world, sometimes out of curiosity, later as a biological necessity, and many times just to feel socially secure. They want to understand one of the primitive fountains and prime urges in life—human relationship. At this stage they seek out equals and similarities and are possessed by the sense of human compatibility. After some initial experimentation, they may realize they are not capable of enjoying anything because their inner strength has been robbed by the foolish behavior of their parents. They neither feel confident and free nor strong and capable. These insecurities of children are reflections shared by their parents in the name of love. If a child has not been properly cared for by either the mother or the father at all the critical stages of development, when the child grows up, he or she will project those unmet needs onto his or her spouse. For such a person, the husband or wife becomes the father or mother respectively. This leads to lifelong incompatibility. What a pitiable situation— two hearts never united, even though they live together. I don't mean that children should be very dependent on their parents. To learn to let go is actually an important part of childhood training. A child who is given his due share of love in childhood will grow up to be a good, healthy person, whose ability to communicate will help him or her to create a healthy, loving family life of his or her own. The cycle continues, and parents are responsible for setting it in motion.

The home is meant for you and your family to learn how to love. And that love should then expand to your community, to your nation, to all other nations, and ultimately to the whole world. Unfortunately, the home that is meant to radiate love has instead become a center of hatred. When you hate each other even in your small homes, what can you expect from yourselves as far as love is concerned? It is very important to modify the basic education that parents impart to their children at home. If your generation is suffering, why should the next generation also suffer? When you understand that you are suffering on account of certain complexes that have come from hatred and selfishness, why do you want your children to also suffer? At home try to become examples for your children so that they also learn to love. Within yourselves try not to create any hatred because hatred hinders your growth. In love one is selfless and does not expect anything in return at all. This is not impossible. When you truly love your children, you have no expectations that in old age they are going to return your hospitality, your love, or your care. When you love your children, you want to do everything for them. But you need to expand this feeling. If you feel delight when you help and serve your children, you can do the same for your neighborhood, for your community, for your society, and even for the whole of humanity. Even though you were born in a small family, you have to grow and learn to become more selfless. Once you learn how to become an example in your immediate family and to do your duties for your family members lovingly, then you can experiment in society. I am not telling you to become generous to society, but just to become dutiful. If you improve yourself and you learn to give, there will be fewer problems in your life.

When you give, you have to sacrifice something. To sacrifice is higher and more difficult than to give. You want to give and you should give. That is the only way. According to the great sages love means giving, giving, giving, without expecting any award. Service done toward others is the real expression of love. When you do something for others selflessly and without any expectation, then you go outside the bounds of your individuality. Nothing can change human destiny but love. Through love you can transform the whole of society.

Today the modern world suffers because of too much expectation. Everyone wants to take, but no one wants to give. That is why I say that modern society is still in a primitive state. It has not yet attained the height of a culture in which parents have learned to give selflessly to their children. The drug culture could be completely controlled in a day if all parents would assure their children that they love them. Can you sacrifice some of your pleasures for your children so they can grow up without any faults? If parents do not teach their children to be selfless, how will they learn selflessness? They may learn the techniques of how to work in the world; they may become great scientists and doctors, great poets and artists, but there will be no love. Such a society will crumble like a house of cards crumbles at the touch of a finger. We all have to think seriously about this.

The moment an individual understands that he did not receive love in childhood, that individual should learn to love others. By loving others you can make up for that and you can forget it. Even if your parents did not love you properly in your childhood, you can still love others and become an example for others. I do not remember my mother or my father. I never think of them or wonder why I did not have a mother and father. And I don't have any psychological problems today. My teacher loved me immensely and selflessly. No child today receives that love which I received in my childhood from my master. I am very proud of it. When I was leaving to begin my work in the West, I said to him, "Sir, you have done everything selflessly for me. What can I do for you? Shall I get a glass of water and sit at your feet with folded hands?" He smiled and said, "Many times I have sat at your feet, my son. Don't go toward these fake rituals." I said, "What can I do for you?" He said, "The way I have loved you, love others in the same way." To this date, I assure you that I am trying my best. But I am not perfect. The highest of all joys in life is that time when I can do something for somebody. If I have money, I quietly give it with a smile and enjoy. I want to see everyone smiling; I want to see everyone healthy and happy.

Many parents become very protective toward their children. A child needs not only protection, but also love—exemplary love. Children are hungry for warmth and love. If you want to have children, you should first learn how to be parents. To be parents means to learn to sacrifice for your children. A Sanskrit verse says you should love your children unconditionally up to the age of five. After the age of five children need both love and discipline. When you love them, love them without any reservation. And sacrifice your pleasures for the sake of that love. If you really want your children to grow properly, learn to sacrifice your personal interests. The actual foundation of the process of human growth is love.

Do you know why you have children? So that you can feel the love of the Lord. A child is a great joy and can teach you the greatest lesson in life. Do you know how much God loves you? Only those who have children can know. *Oh, perhaps God loves me exactly as I love my child.* Those who do not have children cannot feel this. *The way I love my child, the way I can protect my child, the way I can sacrifice for my child, so God also loves me, because I am His child.* You cannot know how God loves you unless you have a child to love. You can really be in tune with your higher Self by having a child and loving your child.

CHAPTER SEVEN

SPIRITUALITY

WITH THE PASSAGE OF TIME, the noble culture of our society has become polluted, and religion, an essential part of culture, has become enveloped by the dust of ignorance. Are religions and blind faith truly helpful or are they something we create because of the insecurity and fear in which we live all the time? Is so-called religion of any value in our daily life? Does it have any function while we are eating, drinking, bathing, and performing other daily duties? I am not against true religion and its codes of conduct, but I am opposed to rigid dogmas that continue to thwart the destiny of human life.

We talk of God; we do kirtan; we study the scriptures; we go to church or temple. Yet, our ignorance remains the same. Nothing changes in our daily life or in our behavior. What is the reason? From our childhood onward we are trained to see and examine things in the external world. Nobody teaches us how to look within, to find within, or to see within. All branches of education inspire and educate us to understand things in the external world, but no one teaches us to look within.

I started teaching when I was very young. If you live in a particular environment, you behave according to that environment. Because I lived in an atmosphere where old swamis used to teach people, I also started teaching, and that became a part of my life. At the age of twenty-three, I sat down one day and thought, *What is this thing called knowledge? There is something intense within me and that power always wants to know something more, and more, and more. It is never-ending. What is this knowledge? What knowledge do I have? I have received knowledge from my teachers, from my friends, from my neighbors, and from my college and university, yet, still I am ignorant. Is it possible that whatever I have received is not really knowledge?*

So I went to my teacher. He said, "You are thinking rightly. Go and think about it some more and then let me know what you have learned." It took me seven days to understand that all the knowledge that we receive from the outside world is only information; it merely informs us of something. If you study and analyze the knowledge that you have, suddenly you will realize that you know nothing; the knowledge that you think you have is not yours. Whatever knowledge you have today, you have received from outside, and most of that knowledge has not gone through the process of filtration: *How much shall I accept of what you say, and how much shall I not accept?* Whatever you have known so far, either you have known from your parents, from your relatives, from your neighbors, or from your schools. But what do you actually know? You will have to say, "I am sorry. I do not know anything."

When you grow and become aware of this reality, suddenly you find that throughout your life you have been learning from others, but that which is called self-learning is not there. So what have you really known? When you do not have something of your own, what do you do? You become dependent on others. And once you start to become dependent on others, it becomes impossible for you to live without others. Even if you have decided to do something, you still go to a priest or to someone else and say, "I am going to do this. Is it okay?" You want confirmation from someone else because you are dependent on others. You are always looking for someone else to teach you something and you remain dependent on other persons. You don't understand that there is a source within you, and that when you come to understand, to know, and to realize that source, you will be enlightened.

The educational systems in both the East and the West focus on educating only the conscious mind—the part of the mind that we ordinarily use in our daily life during the waking state. That is why we are confused. The conscious mind is a very small part of the totality of the mind. We have such a vast, infinite library within us, but our education does not help us to have control over the totality of the mind. The wealth is there, but we do not know in which corner it is buried. We have yet to know the greater part of the mind that lies beneath the level of the conscious mind. Until we learn to utilize that vast portion of the mind, we will remain deprived. All the conflicts in the various elements of society, in the family, and within one's own self, exist because we do not know ourselves on all levels.

In today's schools children are not taught that the mind is different from the brain. The mind is an instrument. You have to train the mind. The more you train the mind, the more you train yourself, and the more you will find that you have dynamic powers within. You do not receive this training from colleges or universities. Universities teach you how to read this language and that language, history, geography, and other academic subjects. But universities rarely teach you how to think. Education today teaches you only to imitate. You are expected to be able to do only what your elders can do. This hampers the full development of the young mind, of which the possibilities are unlimited. This superficial education is not helpful for knowing oneself within. There is another higher education for knowing *paravidya*—that which is beyond. This possibility can be realized only through meditation, which unfortunately our educational systems do not teach.

Although scientific knowledge of the world in which we live is essential to education, for the balanced development of the human personality two currents of thoughts are necessary—the scientific and the spiritual. The modern world today has surrendered itself before material science. Science and technology have reduced physical distances and have brought people from different parts of the world nearer to one another. But the mere study of science without spirituality is leading the rising generation to dehumanization. By exposing our children to a ceaseless barrage of propaganda, we are turning them into precise and predictable machines.

The human being is still incomplete—an unfinished being. It is necessary today for human beings everywhere to become aware of the spiritual potential within. Everyone must take some time to understand his or her inner strength. I am not talking about brute strength; I am talking about the strength that comes from love and gentleness. One who is gentle and who loves others is a strong person; one who is self-centered and egotistical is a weak person. The more egotistical and selfish a person is, the weaker is that person. The more generous and giving a person is, the stronger is that person. Only one who has something to give can give; one who has nothing to give, can give nothing.

When you practice meditation, initially you come in touch with yourself and all your thought patterns; you come to understand your inner dialogue. Then, you learn to discriminate—to select and reject; and finally, you learn how to work with yourself. These seeds should be sown in childhood.

Instead, believers of all faiths, clinging to external rituals, impose their ideals on their children and force them to participate in their time-honored customs. Children are taught to love and to worship pictures of Christ, Krishna, or other gods and goddesses, and sometimes even community or religious leaders. This does not help them to become independent or to acquire peace of mind. Children need to be taught how to cultivate divine virtues within themselves; they need to be taught how to look within, and how to find within in order to attain freedom. I think if everyone were to be given a spiritual education in childhood, they would have fewer problems living in the world. Without understanding the values of spirituality, with all its currents and crosscurrents, one becomes lost living in this jungle that is called world. The world is the real jungle; that which is considered to be the jungle is not the real jungle.

Most diseases originate in childhood. Children become ill because they have not learned the means of acquiring peace of mind. Why do you not lead your children to silence before they learn to be active? Mothers can do this if they are friends with their children. But these days mothers have no time. They go out and enjoy themselves while their children remain at home. The lack of communication between the younger generation and the parents is creating great chaos. First of all, you have to learn to respect the family institution where parents become counselors to their children, and where children accept their parents, not only as parents, but also as friends.

When you make meditation a part of your life, your children will follow your example. Exemplary education is very important for children. Children imitate their parents; you don't have to teach them to meditate. Never do that. You should teach your children through example how to sit quietly and make their minds one-pointed. When you sit in meditation, your child will also come and sit next to you and pretend to do what you are doing. In this way the child will come to know what you are doing and will also form the habit of sitting with you.

I used to do that in my childhood. When my master would sit in meditation, I would sit next to him. When I wanted his attention, I would climb onto his lap. He wouldn't say anything to me, so I would do something to get his attention. Then he would rub my forehead, and I did not know what had happened. I am sure I was not sleeping. If you sit in meditation, and your child comes and sits next to you and closes his eyes, it is very helpful for the child. Do you think the child is meditating? I say the child is meditating better than you are. Even when a child simply imitates you when you are meditating, it is very helpful for the child.

Meditation is a very powerful thing that gives helpful vibrations to all. When you meditate, it definitely affects your children. If you record the brain waves of a child who is sleeping while you are meditating, you will find a difference. Even your plants and your pets are affected when you meditate. Instead of imposing your ego or your emotional problems on your children in the name of discipline, please discipline yourself, and then your children will also learn.

As a part of our educational training we must define spirituality in its most precise and universal terms. Spirituality means that which helps us to discipline our thoughts, speech, and actions; that which leads us toward the center of consciousness, and thereby helps to unfold our inner potentials. Education based on such spiritual guidelines will help humanity to become self-reliant and confident. Only education based on spirituality can bring harmonious balance to both our external and inner life.

We need not force children to believe that there is a God. However, we should provide them with the opportunity to unfold their inner potentials, to gain confidence, and to become inspired to search for God according to their own inner tendencies and capacity. For children to learn to cultivate divine virtues within themselves, the knowledge of theories that prove the existence of God is not as important as to learn how to discipline oneself. Through self-discipline God can be experienced directly.

Spiritual practices, undertaken at an early age, have a profound and long lasting effect. Human beings have tremendous potential provided they are taught to train themselves on all levels—physical, mental, and spiritual. Let us teach our children how to become aware of themselves on all levels. With a calm and one-pointed mind, children can obtain a glimpse of true peace and happiness.

CHAPTER EIGHT

CONCLUSION

IF THERE IS TO BE any higher civilization in the world, it will start from family life. The family institution is higher than all temples, churches, and synagogues. Householders are the real foundation of society. If you are a householder, do not feel that your role is inferior. Your role in society is not only to express your biological needs or emotional needs, but also to establish the fundamentals of society so that the whole of society attains a state of peace and happiness. The world will attain the next civilization of enlightenment when all of humanity understands that the home is meant to radiate love to other families. The home should never radiate hatred, jealousy, or other bad feelings. The home is meant to establish and maintain peace, so that one can enjoy love and radiate love to others. When all human beings become aware of this reality, there will be joy everywhere. And when there will be joy everywhere, there will be nothing to disturb your mind. Then your mind will automatically travel upward to the center of consciousness from where consciousness flows on various degrees and grades.

Let us try our best to reconstruct our society. We are the custodians of our culture; we have to build this culture; we have to be examples. If one person is liberated, society does not gain anything; if one person becomes a monk and attains liberation, it does not benefit society. No matter how many great leaders and gods come, no one can help us if we are not prepared to help ourselves. What we need is liberation of the masses. Everyone has to become liberated. This can be done if you accept your duties and learn to do your duties with love. Then you will not be a slave to your duties and you will enjoy doing them. You are a slave to your duties when you feel you have to do them. You frequently say, "I really don't want to do it, but I have to." This is not the right way to live. To enjoy life means to learn to love your duties so those duties give you freedom and a sense of joy and happiness. You can start by loving your children. As you love your children, you can slowly learn to expand and extend that love to other people in your society.

The orthodox way of raising a child is based on a sense of false identity, and the Western way is based on psychological and biological curiosity. Both methods are imperfect. Mothers should sit together and devise something new, neither forgetting the ancient nor ignoring modern scientific discoveries, but adding something more vital so that the child's upbringing becomes a joy for both the child and the mother.

Children are the real gods, and they should be revered with full attention, love, and adoration. We have to impart good education to all children because they are the fathers and mothers of the next generation of our society. Parents have to be especially careful with the education they impart to their children in the home, for society is an expansion of family life. Parents should give single-pointed devotion and attention to every child they have. If parents would pay full attention to their children in early childhood, give them tender loving care, and allow them to grow according to their inborn tendencies, our society would be full of creative geniuses who have the capacity to love, to share, and to be aware of the reality of coexistence—the philosophy of "Live and let live." If we transmit this philosophy to our children, they will hear the cry of peace, and there will be actual peace here, there, and everywhere.

Childhood is the best of all periods in life, and it never returns. Children are the most beautiful flowers; they can make our society bloom. Without children no nation can survive. We need the help of children who have been loved, well cared for, and wisely educated, if we really want to improve society. There is no better foundation for a happy life than a happy childhood.

About the Author

SWAMI RAMA was born in the Himalayas and was initiated by his master into many yogic practices. In addition, he sent Swamiji to other yogis and adepts of the Himalayas to gain new perspectives and insights into the ancient teachings. At the young age of twenty-four he was installed as Shankaracharya of Karvirpitham in South India. Swamiji relinquished this position to pursue intense sadhana in the caves of the Himalayas. Having successfully completed this sadhana, he was directed by his master to go to Japan and to the West in order to illustrate the scientific basis of the ancient yogic practices. At the Menninger Foundation in Topeka, Kansas, Swamiji convincingly demonstrated the capacity of the mind to control so-called involuntary physiological processes such as the heart rate, temperature, and brain waves. Swamiji's work in the United States continued for twenty-three years, and in this period he established the Himalayan International Institute.

Swamiji became well recognized in the States as a yogi, teacher, philosopher, poet, humanist, and philanthropist. His models of preventive medicine, holistic health, and stress management have permeated the mainstream of western mediicne. In

1989 Swamiji returned to India where he established the Himalayan Institute Hospital Trust in the foothills of the Garhwal Himalayas. Swamiji left this physical plane in November, 1996, but the seeds he has sown continue to sprout, bloom, and bear fruit. His teachings, embodied in the words, "Love, Serve, Remember," continue to inspire the many students whose good fortune it was to come in contact with such an accomplished, selfless, and loving master.

HIMALAYAN INSTITUTE HOSPITAL TRUST

PERHAPS THE MOST visible form of Swami Rama's service to humanity is the Himalayan Institute Hospital Trust (HIHT). HIHT is a nonprofit organization committed to the premise that all human beings have the right to health, education, and economic self-sufficiency. The comprehensive health care and social development programs of HIHT incorporate medical care, education, and research. The philosophy of HIHT is: love, serve, and remember.

The mission of the Trust is to develop integrated and cost-effective approaches to health care and development that address the local population, and which can serve as a model for the country as a whole, and for the underserved population worldwide. A combined approach in which traditional systems of health care complement modern medicine and advanced technology is the prime focus of clinical care, medical education, and research at HIHT.

HIHT is located in the state of Uttarakhand, one of the underdeveloped states of India. A bold vision to bring medical services to the millions of people in northern India, many of whom are underprivileged and have little or no health care, began modestly in

1989 with a small outpatient department. Today it is the site of a world class medical city and educational campus that includes: a large state-of-the-art hospital offering a full range of medical specialities and services, a holistic health program, a deemed university, a school of nursing, a rural development institute, and accommodations for staff, students, and patients' families. This transformation is the result of the vision of Sri Swami Rama.

For information contact:
Himalayan Institute Hospital Trust
Swami Ram Nagar, P.O. Doiwala
Distt. Dehradun 248140, Uttarakhand, India
Phone: 91-135-247-1133, Fax: 91-135-247-1122
pb@hihtindia.org, www.hihtindia.org

Swami Rama Foundation of the USA, Inc.

The Swami Rama Foundation of the USA is a registered, nonprofit and tax-exempt organization committed to the vision of the Indian sage Swami Rama. The Foundation was established to provide financial assistance and technical support to institutions and individuals who are ready to implement this vision in the USA and abroad. The essence of Swami Rama's vision lies in bridging the gap between Western Science and Eastern Wisdom through the integration of mind, body, and spirit.

For information contact: Swami Rama Foundation of the USA, Inc., 2410 N. Farwell Avenue, Milwaukee, WI 53211, USA. Phone 414-273-1621, info@swamiramafoundation.us

Sadhana
The Essence of Spiritual Life
a companion guide for the seeker
Swami Rama

This concise collection of Swami Rama's
teachings serves as a practical guide for the
spiritual seeker. Spiritual practice leads the
seeker towards inner experiences of
divinity that further one towards attaining the goal of life.
Swami Rama, yogi, scientist, philosopher and humanitarian,
was deeply steeped in the spiritual traditions of the Himalayan
sages. He was a free thinker, guided by direct experience and
inner wisdom. His teachings are universal and nonsectarian,
providing a bridge between the East and the West.

ISBN 978-190100-49-6; Rs. 150, paperback, 136 pages

SAMADHI
the Higest State of Wisdom
Yoga the Sacred Science, volume one
Swami Rama

Samadhi: The Highest State of Wisdom brings
Patanjali's Yoga Sutras to life in a very
personal and helpful way.

Swami Rama's description of the totality
of the mind, the functions of the mind, and
the emotions, goes far beyond the concepts of modern
psychology, and provides insight into the intricacies of yoga
psychology, making this an invaluable edition from the
therapeutic viewpoint as well as its practicality as a guide for
living a healthy, balanced life.

ISBN 978-81-88157-36-5; Rs. 175, paperback, 256 pages

Conscious Living
A Guidebook for Spiritual Transformation
Swami Rama

This is a practical book for people living in the world. The word "practical" implies that the teaching can be practiced in the world, in the midst of family, career and social obligations. No prior preparation is required for reading this book, and after reading this book, no further teaching is required. If one were to sincerely practice the teachings presented by Sri Swami Rama in this book, one will surely achieve the goal of self-realization, a state described by Swamiji as the summum bonum of life, a state of bliss, a state of perfection.

ISBN 978-81-88157-03-7, Rs. 120, paperback, 160 pages

Conscious Living
An Audiobook for Spiritual Transformation
Swami Rama

This 5-CD set is a collection of lectures that Swami Rama gave in Singapore in 1991 and 1992. Recorded live, they capture the essence and inspiration of Swamiji's public speaking style. His book, *Conscious Living: A Guidebook for Spiritual Transformation* is derived from nine of the lectures he presented in Singapore. Five of those lectures are included in this new audiobook.

Volume one: Prayer, Meditation, Contemplation, 56.40 minutes
Volume two: Freedom from Stress, 57.45 minutes
Volume three: Creative Use of Emotions, 62.01 minutes
Volume four: Mind and its Modifications, 45.31 minutes
Volume five: The Goal of Life, 43.08 minutes

Available in CD or cassette format. Each CD Rs. 150, each cassette Rs. 60. Ten percent discount for purchasing entire set at one time.